STECK-VAUGHN

PORTRAIT OF AMERICA

South Carolina

Steck-Vaughn Company

Executive Editor	Diane Sharpe
Senior Editor	Martin S. Saiewitz
Design Manager	Pamela Heaney
Photo Editor	Margie Foster

Proof Positive/Farrowlyne Associates, Inc.
Program Editorial, Revision Development, Design, and Production

Consultant: Allison L. Harrill, Public Information Coordinator, State Ombudsman Staff

Published by Raintree Steck-Vaughn Publishers, an imprint of Steck-Vaughn Company.

A Turner Educational Services, Inc. book. Based on the Portrait of America television series by R. E. (Ted) Turner.

Cover Photo: Swamp at Magnolia Plantation by © Gerald Fritz/FPG.

Library of Congress Cataloging-in-Publication Data

Thompson, Kathleen.
    South Carolina / Kathleen Thompson.
       p.   cm. — (Portrait of America)
    "A Turner book."
    "Based on the Portrait of America television series"—T.p. verso.
    Includes index.
    ISBN 0-8114-7386-4 (library binding).—ISBN 0-8114-7467-4 (softcover)
    1. South Carolina—Juvenile literature. I. Title. II. Series:
Thompson, Kathleen. Portrait of America.
F269.3.T48 1996
975.7—dc20

                                            95-40011
                                             CIP
                                           AC

Acknowledgments
The publishers wish to thank the following for permission to reproduce photographs:
P. 7 © Michael Reagan; p. 8 The Bettmann Archive; pp. 9, 10 South Caroliana Library; p. 13 Boone Hall; p. 14 South Caroliana Library; p. 15 South Carolina Department of Agriculture; p. 16 (top) Beineke Rare Book and Manuscript Library, Yale University, (bottom) South Caroliana Library; p. 17 South Caroliana Library; p. 19 © Russ Pace/The Citadel; p. 20 South Carolina Department of Parks, Recreation, & Tourism; p. 21 (top) UPI/Bettmann, (bottom) Reuters/Bettmann; p. 22 (both) The Bettmann Archive; pp. 23, 25 The Historical Society of Pennsylvania; p. 26 Abbeville Historic Preservation Commission; p. 27 Museum of the Confederacy Collection; p. 28 Charleston Port Authority; p. 30 Springs Industries, Inc.; pp. 31 (both), 32 South Carolina Department of Agriculture; p. 33 Hilton Head Convention and Visitors Bureau; p. 35 (top) © Jeff Anberg/Midlands Technical College, (bottom) Midlands Technical College; p. 36 © G. Humphries/Midlands Technical College; p. 36 © Superstock; p. 38 (top) Charleston Ballet Theatre, (bottom) Charleston Convention & Visitors Bureau; p. 39 (top) Institute of Jazz, Rutgers University, (bottom) South Carolina Department of Parks, Recreation, & Tourism; p. 41 (top) © Wade Spees/McKissick Museum, (bottom) Lowcountry & Resort Islands Tourism Commission; p. 42 © Karl Weatherly/Tony Stone Images; p. 44 © Phillip Jones/South Carolina Department of Natural Resources; p. 46 One Mile Up; p. 47 (left) One Mile Up, (middle, right) South Carolina Department of Parks, Recreation, & Tourism.

STECK-VAUGHN

PORTRAIT OF AMERICA

South Carolina

Kathleen Thompson

A Turner Book

RSVP
RAINTREE
STECK-VAUGHN
PUBLISHERS
The Steck-Vaughn Company

Austin, Texas

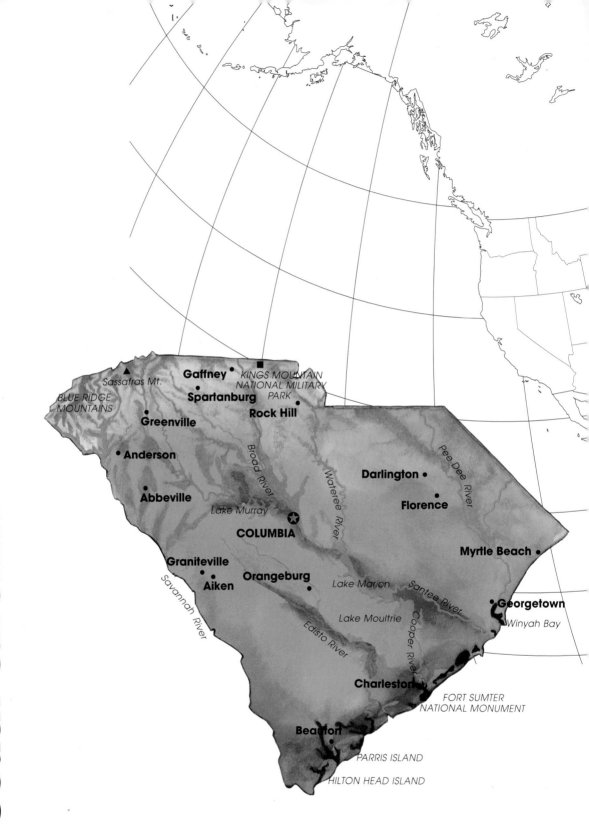

South Carolina

Sassafras Mt.

BLUE RIDGE
MOUNTAINS

Gaffney

Spartanburg

KINGS MOUNTAIN
NATIONAL MILITARY
PARK

Greenville

Rock Hill

Anderson

Broad River

Wateree River

Darlington

Pee Dee River

Florence

Abbeville

Lake Murray

COLUMBIA

Myrtle Beach

Graniteville

Aiken

Orangeburg

Lake Marion

Santee River

Lake Moultrie

Georgetown

Winyah Bay

Savannah River

Edisto River

Cooper River

Charleston

FORT SUMTER
NATIONAL MONUMENT

Beaufort

PARRIS ISLAND

HILTON HEAD ISLAND

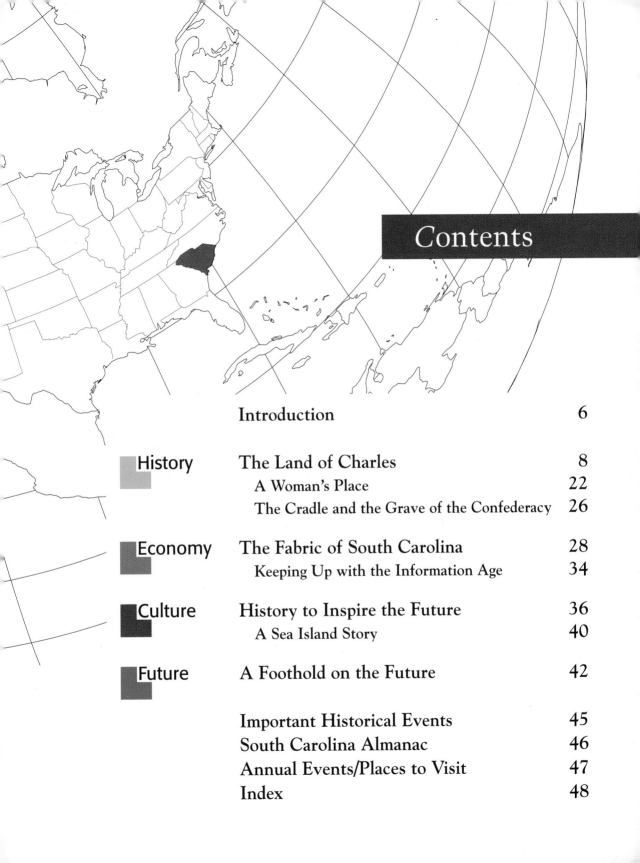

Contents

Introduction

Visiting South Carolina is a bit like traveling through time. That's because in South Carolina you can still glimpse its long, complex history. Elegant pre-Civil War mansions adorn broad green lawns. Vast fields of cotton extend for miles. These things are still present. They call to mind a time when life seemed slower-paced and simpler. Although South Carolina cherishes its past, it has also learned from it. Today, South Carolina is anything but simple. From industry to antipollution laws, South Carolina has become a leader. It wears its past like an emblem; a southern state of the United States entering a new century.

Charleston, South Carolina, is a mix of old and new. Besides modern buildings, it has 73 buildings that date from before the Revolutionary War, 136 from the late 1700s, and more than 600 from before 1840.

South Carolina

...ntations, textiles, the Palmetto State

The Land of Charles

Before Europeans came to the land that is now called South Carolina, almost fifty Native American groups lived there. The largest were the Catawba, Cherokee, and Yamassee. There is also evidence of even earlier inhabitants. Many scholars believe that people lived in the area as far back as 25,000 years ago. By 1000 B.C., Native Americans in this area began farming to supplement their hunting and fishing. They grew corn, beans, and squash. Most of them used wood, bark, grass, and palmetto leaves to build their homes.

The first European explorers arrived in 1521 at the mouth of Winyah Bay, near present-day Georgetown. They were led ashore by a Spaniard named Francisco Gordillo. He and his crew were from Santo Domingo, a Spanish island southeast of Florida in what is now called the West Indies.

Five years later, Lucas Vásquez de Ayllón, also from Santo Domingo, brought five hundred Spanish settlers to Winyah Bay. But they were unable to adapt

Francis Marion was a leader of a South Carolina militia during the Revolutionary War. He led raids against the British, sometimes capturing supplies or rescuing American prisoners.

The Carolinas were named after King Charles I. Charles was executed in England in 1649, when his rule was overthrown after a civil war.

to the different way of life, including new diseases and a new climate. Many of them died. After a few months, 150 survivors of the expedition returned to Spain.

Some years later, the French also attempted to settle in the area. In about 1562 a short-lived settlement was established by Jean Ribaut on Parris Island. The Spanish tried again in 1566. This time the settlement lasted for about ten years. Disease and battles with Native Americans eventually forced the settlers to give up and return to Europe.

The English, who also claimed this land, would succeed where the Spanish and French had failed. In 1629 King Charles I of England gave present-day North and South Carolina to his friend

and subject, Sir Robert Heath. King Charles declared that Heath had the right to colonize this area. It came to be called *Carolana*, which meant "the land of Charles."

Heath did nothing with the land; he sent no one over to colonize it. So in 1663 King Charles II took back the land from Heath and gave it to eight of his friends who were more ambitious. These eight men were called the lords proprietor.

The lords proprietor immediately began to recruit settlers for the land. About one hundred arrived in March 1670 at a spot called Albemarle Point. They named their settlement Charles Towne. Ten years later these settlers moved to a peninsula about three miles away, between the Ashley and Cooper rivers. It is the site of today's Charleston.

The new settlers didn't care that the area was already occupied by Native Americans. In fact, the settlers tried to enslave some of them. As a result,

This painting shows Charleston Harbor as it was around 1740, about fifty years after the city was established.

fighting broke out between the settlers and the Native Americans. The most significant attacks were by the Yamassee, beginning in 1715. The settlers eventually defeated them and drove them south into what is now Florida, but the colony was left in ruins. The lords proprietor did little or nothing to help their settlers during the attacks. The settlers were having other problems as well. The area was constantly being raided by pirates! The famous Blackbeard and other pirates repeatedly destroyed towns along the coast. Again, the lords refused to send help for the settlers.

In 1719 the colonists rebelled against the lords proprietor. They asked King George I to make the Carolinas a royal colony. In 1729 the king took back the South Carolina area from the eight noblemen, and he created separate royal governments for North Carolina and South Carolina.

Two very different lifestyles began to develop in South Carolina. The eastern coastal area came to be known as the Low Country. The farmers in this area raised rice and indigo, a plant used to make blue dye. The large plantations in the Low Country used slave labor. In fact they had so many slaves that by 1720 the colony had almost twice as many African slaves as free people. The plantation owners enjoyed a luxurious lifestyle.

Farther inland, in an area called the Up Country, were small farms. The Up Country farmers had little in common with the rich planters of the Low Country. Many of them had to struggle to feed their families. They could not afford to purchase slaves. The Up

These people are making baskets in front of a former slave cabin at the Boone Hall plantation, near Charleston. During the slave-trade years, an estimated 15 million Africans were brought to the Americas, while another four million died during the voyage.

Country planters began to get angry that the Low Country planters held all the positions in the colonial government.

In 1763 Great Britain started passing laws that limited the rights of the colonies to trade with other countries. The British also put high taxes on goods that the colonists needed. The Up Country people were not as harshly affected by these laws as those in the Low Country. This is because they did not purchase as many of the taxed goods as the Low Country people did. Many of the Up Country people wanted to remain loyal to Great Britain. The Low Country planters had control of the local government, however. When the colonists began to openly rebel, South Carolina sent delegates to the Continental Congress. They later signed the Declaration of Independence.

The British attacked Charleston in 1776. The patriots won this round, but the British succeeded in taking over the city when they tried again in 1780.

The Revolutionary War began in Massachusetts in 1775. The fighting reached South Carolina in June 1776, when the British attempted to capture Charleston. Soldiers in a small fort on Sullivans Island in Charleston Harbor held them off. The fort, later called Fort Moultrie, was made of palmetto logs. The defense of this fort inspired South Carolina's nickname, the Palmetto State. About 25,000 South Carolinian patriots fought in the Revolutionary War. However, many people in the colony remained loyal to Great Britain. Small battles continually broke out between patriot and loyalist South Carolinians.

The British succeeded in capturing Charleston in 1780. But the patriots refused to give up. South

Carolinians won a number of battles using fighting tactics that the British were not used to. The soldiers hid in the mountains and swamps and ambushed the British when they were not expecting it. The most famous of these soldiers was Francis Marion. He was called the Swamp Fox because of the way he tricked the British in battles that took place in his native swamplands.

In late 1780, the patriots stopped the British at Kings Mountain. They won another victory at Cowpens a year later. The tide of the war began to turn. The British eventually abandoned Charleston, and in 1783 the war ended. On May 23, 1788, South Carolina became the eighth state to approve the Constitution of the new United States of America.

After the war, South Carolina's small farmers and plantation owners returned to growing their crops. Most of them had grown rice and indigo, but that changed. In 1793 a machine called the cotton gin was invented. This machine removed cotton seeds quickly, which cut labor costs and made cotton crops much more profitable. Now that cotton could be grown cheaper than other crops, plantation owners in South Carolina and all across the South started growing mainly cotton. "King Cotton" became the economic backbone of the South. More slaves than ever before were needed to harvest this crop as it became more widespread.

South Carolina's economic success spurred a feeling of independence. They did not like the federal government's growing list of laws and restrictions.

At the height of the "King Cotton" era, cotton made up over half of the exports in all of the United States.

When the federal government raised taxes on trade in 1832, South Carolinians, led by Senator John C. Calhoun, passed their own law. It stated that the taxes were "null and void," meaning people in South Carolina didn't have to pay them. President Andrew Jackson threatened to send troops to make them obey the new tax laws. Congress eventually gave in and lowered the taxes, so South Carolina repealed its "nullification" law.

By 1850 South Carolina had four hundred thousand slaves. This was almost two thirds of the state's entire population. Plantation owners all over the South worried about slave uprisings. The antislavery movement was gaining power. Plantation owners in South Carolina's Low Country were angry and frightened. Their plantations and their rich lifestyles depended on slave labor. Abraham Lincoln's election

to the Presidency in 1860 was the last straw for many South Carolinians. The state seceded, or withdrew, from the Union on December 2, 1860. Ten other southern states soon followed its example. These states formed the Confederate States of America.

The country was thrust into war once again. The first clash of the Civil War took place on April 12, 1861. Confederate troops in South Carolina fired on the Union's Fort Sumter in Charleston Harbor and captured it in a matter of days. During the course of the war, over sixty thousand soldiers from South Carolina went into battle. Almost a quarter of them never returned.

The people at home suffered greatly, too. A Union naval blockade of Charleston made food, medicine, and other important supplies hard to find. In 1865 the Union's General William Tecumseh Sherman led 65,000 troops across the South, burning plantations and towns. Sherman's army nearly destroyed Columbia, the capital of South Carolina. The state was in ruins.

After the war, the defeated Southerners were bitter. Perhaps Abraham Lincoln could have guided

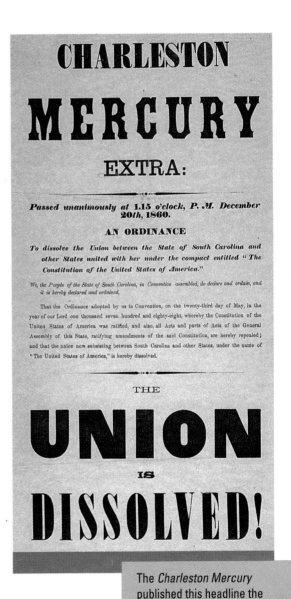

The *Charleston Mercury* published this headline the day after South Carolina's secession.

the country wisely and compassionately through the postwar period, called Reconstruction. Only a few days after the end of the war, however, Lincoln was assassinated by a Confederate sympathizer named John Wilkes Booth.

Over four hundred thousand slaves were freed at once after the war. Although they were glad to be free, they were without homes or jobs. Since they were free, however, they could now vote, run for office, and be represented in the government. The Freedmen's Bureau was set up by Congress to aid former slaves by providing schools, legal help, and assistance in obtaining land or employment. But violence and discrimination against African Americans continued. Groups were formed to keep African Americans away from the voting booths.

When African Americans were elected to public office for the first time, many Southerners became afraid of their power. In 1890 Benjamin R. Tillman was elected governor of South Carolina. He sponsored a new state constitution that robbed African American citizens of their right to vote. The inequalities started by politicians such as Tillman were not repaired in South Carolina for almost 75 years. These inequalities took shape in what are known as the Jim Crow laws. These were legal obstacles, such as complicated voting requirements, put in the path of African Americans to keep them from participating in the election system. In 1882 South Carolina adopted the Eight Box law that required voting ballots for separate offices or candidates to be placed in separate boxes.

The Citadel, a military college in Charleston, opened in 1842. It is one of the last two state-supported military colleges in the nation.

This was a difficult task for anyone who could not read or write, as many African Americans could not.

Many difficult economic changes also took place in the state. From 1914 to 1918, South Carolina's textile industry boomed. But the economy fell once again in the 1920s when a bug called the boll weevil ruined almost half of the state's cotton crop. The Great Depression of the 1930s brought even more hardship. Many people were struggling to survive economically. President Franklin D. Roosevelt's policies eased the country's financial burden somewhat. After the United States became involved in World War II in the 1940s, factories were reopened to make products for the war

The 350-seat Abbeville Opera House was built in 1908 and has recently been restored.

effort. Military bases reopened, also. Manufacturing materials for the war effort slowly brought prosperity back to the state. South Carolina began to enter a new stage in its history.

Improvements in South Carolina's African American communities came about more slowly. In 1948 African Americans in the state were no longer restricted from voting. But when the United States Supreme Court ruled in 1954 that having separate schools for African Americans was unconstitutional, the South Carolina legislature became stubborn. Rather than have children of different races go to school together, it passed a bill in 1955 that said that children no longer had to attend school at all. Children in South Carolina were not required to attend school until 1967. By 1970 the state finally began to uphold the rest of the country's laws concerning equal education for all Americans.

Schools across the state became integrated, which means they were attended by students of all races. In 1983 I. DeQuincey Newman became the first African American to be elected to South Carolina's Senate in almost one hundred years.

In the 1980s, residents of Aiken found out that nuclear power plants built there in the 1950s had been leaking. Three reactors were shut down in 1988. The work required to clean up the community and its surrounding environment is expected to last into the twenty-first century.

In 1989 Hurricane Hugo struck the East Coast. The storm killed 180 people and destroyed about forty thousand homes in South Carolina. Rebuilding projects were completed by the mid-1990s, and Charleston and other coastal towns are thriving once again.

James Strom Thurmond has served in the United States Senate since 1954.

The owners of these boats thought the boats would be safe from Hurricane Hugo in the Isle of Palms Harbor, near Charleston. Unfortunately, hurricane winds reached 135 miles per hour in the Charleston area, and the boats were wrecked.

A Woman's Place

"A woman's place is in the House—and the Senate!" proclaims a current bumper sticker. But in the early 1800s, when Sarah and Angelina Grimké were born, a woman's role was no joke. Women of that time were expected—even required—to stay at home.

Even a woman's home was not her own. Married women had no legal rights over their property, their earnings, or even their own children. They could not vote. Their education was strictly limited. Women in those days were not expected to work outside the home.

If a woman did manage to find a job, her wages were less than half what a man would earn at the same

After the Grimké sisters moved to Philadelphia, Angelina Grimké began addressing small groups of women in private homes.

Sarah Grimké was one of the first American women to publish a statement on the equality of the sexes.

Angelina Grimké's Appeal to the Christian Women of the South was circulated by antislavery organizations.

job. As a result, during this time most women managed their households and became involved in charity. Sarah and Angelina Grimké, however, were not satisfied with this way of life.

Growing up in Charleston, South Carolina, they had seen slavery first-hand, and they were determined to end it. First, they tried to end slavery in their own family. But their efforts were in vain. Their mother would not even open a window herself; she depended on her slaves for everything. Their sisters and brothers defended the way of life they knew. Sarah and Angelina left South Carolina in protest over slavery. They moved north to Philadelphia and joined the antislavery movement there.

In 1835 the Grimké sisters became active members of the Philadelphia Female Anti-Slavery Society. In July a mob attacked the Philadelphia Post

Office and stole sacks of antislavery literature. The sacks were burned along with effigies, or stuffed figures, of famed abolitionist William Lloyd Garrison and others. Angelina wrote a letter to Garrison after she read of that incident, urging him never to give up his ground in the fight against slavery. The next year she wrote a pamphlet entitled *Appeal to the Christian Women of the South*. The pamphlet, which was published in Garrison's newspaper, *The Liberator*, urged southern women to take action against slavery. That same year, the two sisters began a speaking tour of New England. They spoke out against slavery at churches, sewing circles, private parlors, and town halls. They were the first American women to make speeches to the general public. In 1838 they became the first women to address the Massachusetts legislature.

As abolitionists, people who work to abolish slavery, Sarah and Angelina risked jeers, beatings, and jail. As women, they suffered public scorn. Many people at that time believed that women should not speak out in public. The press dubbed them Sarah and "Devilina" Grimké. Journalists often

told them to remember that they were women and they should keep their place as women. Sarah and Angelina replied that women, as well as slaves, should enjoy equal rights. The two women began to work and speak for women's rights in addition to the rights of slaves. In 1837 Angelina wrote another pamphlet called *Appeal to the Women of the Nominally Free States*. A year later, Sarah published her own *Letter on the Equality of the Sexes*. Their pamphlets and speeches inspired men and women across the nation to form abolition societies and to work for equality.

One of the men who was most impressed with their work was the abolitionist Theodore Weld. In 1837 Weld began a correspondence with Angelina Grimké. He read her articles and speeches, offered her advice, and praised her work for women's rights and abolition. In time their letters became more personal. Although he had vowed never to marry until slavery was abolished, Weld confessed to Angelina that he loved her. She answered that she loved him, too.

In 1838 the two reformers married. Together with Sarah, they

The Philadelphia abolition movement made progress due to the efforts of the Grimké sisters and others. However, not everyone was pleased with the abolitionists' work. Pennsylvania Hall, the new home of the Abolition Society, was burned to the ground in May 1838.

continued their mission to lecture and write for freedom and equality. Most people assumed the Welds would retire from public life once they were married. But they continued to speak out against slavery and for women's rights.

Throughout the Civil War, Sarah, Angelina, and Theodore Weld worked for freedom and equality. With the help of other activists, the Grimké sisters showed that a person's place is wherever he—or she—chooses to be of service.

The Cradle and the Grave of the Confederacy

Not many people have heard of Abbeville, South Carolina. But this small town played a very important part in our nation's history. Abbeville is called "the cradle and the grave of the Confederacy." On December 20, 1860, South Carolina officially seceded, or withdrew, from the United States. South Carolina became a leader of the Confederate States of America when it announced its act to the nation in a document called the "secession papers." Less than a month earlier, on November 22, 1860, the secession papers were read to the residents of Abbeville. So many people showed up in the town square that day that the reading had to be moved to a nearby hill. The hill was soon called Secession Hill.

Why is Abbeville also called the Confederacy's "grave"? About four and a half years after the secession, General Robert E. Lee, commander of the Confederate forces, surrendered at Appomattox Court House in Virginia. But the official end of the Confederacy took place a month later—in Abbeville. On May 2, 1865, about a month after Lee's surrender, a meeting was held in the Burt-Stark House in Abbeville. There Jefferson Davis, the president of the Confederacy, formally disbanded

The Burt-Stark House in Abbeville was where the Civil War officially ended.

the War Council of the Confederate Forces. The Burt-Stark House still stands in Abbeville, a favorite stop for South Carolina's visitors.

The history of the Civil War isn't the only segment of the past kept alive in the town. The Abbeville Opera House, built in 1908, has a history of its own. Famous entertainers, such as Groucho Marx, Jimmy Durante, and Fanny Brice, stopped here with their touring variety shows in the early 1900s. The building has recently been restored, and there's a performance almost every night.

The Abbeville County Library holds artifacts from early history. The library has the Poliakoff Collection of Western Art, which boasts one of the largest showcases of Native American art in the South. The collection includes Native American paintings, ceramics, weavings, and bronze artifacts.

As resident George Settles explained, "Abbeville has this richness and energy. Not because of the buildings and not because it's a historic little town—a lot of towns have a lot of history. It's because nobody has allowed that [history] to die." Settles knows what he's talking about—he headed the team that restored the Abbeville Opera House. It's the efforts of such dedicated people that have kept the town's history alive for residents and tourists alike.

The Fabric of South Carolina

If people ever stop sleeping on sheets, wearing clothes, hanging curtains, or upholstering their furniture, the economy of South Carolina would be in trouble. All of these activities of daily life involve textiles—cloth and the fibers used to make cloth. Textiles are South Carolina's major manufacturing industry. Only North Carolina and Georgia produce more textiles. In fact, the town of Greenville, South Carolina, is often called the Textile Center of the World.

In the early 1900s, textiles made from cotton upheld the economy of South Carolina. Now synthetic, or human-made, fabrics lead the field. The production of synthetic textiles helps make the chemical industry the state's second-largest area of manufacturing. Not only do chemical companies make the fibers used in synthetic fabrics, they also make the dyes to color these fabrics. But the chemical industry in South Carolina involves more than textiles. The

Charleston Harbor handles about 8.5 million tons of trade goods a year from the United States and many foreign countries.

South Carolina textile mills weave cotton cloth from giant spools of cotton thread.

government runs a plant in the state that produces chemicals used in the space program. In addition, other chemical plants across the state also make fertilizer.

The third and fourth largest areas of manufacturing are paper and machinery. South Carolina's paper mills make products such as tape and posterboard, in addition to regular paper. The machinery industry is one more industry related to textiles—it produces many of the machines that make thread, weave cloth, and dye fabrics. Other types of machinery, such as hardware and turbines for power plants, are also made in South Carolina's factories.

The economy of South Carolina isn't entirely supported by manufacturing. Farming is still a big part of life in the state. The state's land is taken up by almost six million acres of farms. But agriculture makes up only one percent of South Carolina's gross state product, the value of all its goods and services.

Cotton used to be the major crop in South Carolina. After the boll weevil destroyed half of the state's cotton harvest in the 1920s, farmers were forced to try some new crops. Today, more soybeans, tobacco, and corn are grown in the state than cotton. Peaches are also a major crop. In fact, the only state that raises more peaches than South Carolina is California. Peaches are so important to the town of Gaffney that they built a water tower shaped like a giant peach!

Much of South Carolina's farming income also comes from livestock and poultry. Beef cattle are most important, and dairy cattle come in second. Milk's role in South Carolina's economy has made it the official state beverage.

Seafood has been important to the coastal areas of South Carolina for hundreds of years. Shrimp are the most valuable catch, but South Carolina's crabs, clams, and oysters are also in demand. In all, South Carolina's fishing

South Carolina's peach orchards are mostly in the northern part of the state.

Most of South Carolina's tobacco farms are in the northeastern corner of the state.

boats bring in about $24 million worth of seafood each year.

Fishing is connected to another booming South Carolina industry—tourism. Outdoor enthusiasts fish for bass—the official state fish—along with trout, whiting, and other kinds of fish. Tourists also come to South Carolina for its beach resorts, such as Myrtle Beach and Hilton Head. Historic Revolutionary War and Civil War sites, along with historic cities such as Charleston, are also popular. All these aspects of South Carolina have made tourism the state's second leading industry. In the 1990s, however, tourism declined due to the damage caused by Hurricane Hugo.

Service industries in general are growing in South Carolina. Service industries are industries that provide services to people and businesses instead of producing goods. People who wait on visitors at hotels, gift stores, and information centers are examples of service industry workers in the tourism branch. South Carolina's most important area of service industries, however, is not in tourism but in the government. Military bases, public schools, and hospitals are some examples of governmental service

Much of South Carolina's cotton is grown in small towns between Columbia and Charleston.

industries. All of South Carolina's service industries taken together produce almost three quarters of the state's gross state product.

A final main ingredient of South Carolina's thriving economy is its focus on foreign trade. Many states are just beginning to realize how important foreign trade can be to a healthy economy. Almost half of South Carolina's total investments in manufacturing are from other countries. South Carolina has been helping companies from Japan, the former West Germany, and other countries build plants in the state since as early as the 1970s. Overall, South Carolina has been one of the most successful states in the nation at bringing in foreign investment.

The people of South Carolina have learned how to diversify—to earn their income from many different areas. Now it has one of the strongest economies in the nation.

Hilton Head is one of South Carolina's most popular resort towns. During its peak seasons, it attracts more than 55,000 visitors.

Keeping Up with the Information Age

Times are changing all over the world. Perhaps you've heard that we now live in an "information age." Most people used to work making things you can see and touch. But today more and more people's jobs involve working with information. Many people see this as an exciting change, as their jobs become more and more challenging. To many others, however, the information age can be overwhelming, even frightening.

Part of the reason many people are frightened by this change is that machines are doing the jobs that they used to do. In South Carolina this means that many factory workers, especially in the textile mills, need to find new jobs. Many of these people have been working in factories all their lives, and they have no experience working at any other type of job. That's why schools like Midlands Technical College in Columbia help

Midlands Tech students get plenty of experience doing technical work such as repairing computer boards.

Midlands Technical College works with local businesses and organizations to tailor its programs to community needs.

MIDLANDS TECHNICAL COLLEGE
BELTLINE CAMPUS

these people learn the skills they need to adapt to the changing workplace.

Helping these people takes more than just classes. As Dr. Leroy Brown, former vice president of Midlands Tech, explains, "I see these people in a struggle, trying to survive, their jobs and their job skills taken right from under them. . . . You really have to give them a lot of support and a lot of counseling in order for them to accept what's actually happening to them. And that's been my life—to motivate, to inspire, and to make people feel like they've got a sense of self-worth and a sense of self-dignity."

Students at Midlands Tech get even more than self-respect—they get new jobs. Over ninety percent of graduates are placed either in new positions or in four-year programs at other schools. That's one of the best success rates in the state—maybe even in the nation.

Midlands Tech helps all kinds of people, not just former mill workers. Many students are single parents or homemakers who have never held a full-time job. Most students are between 25 and 30 years old—but not all of them. In 1994 a 70-year-old

One quarter of Midlands Tech graduates return to school to finish a four-year degree.

woman studied practical nursing. That same year a 14-year-old boy took classes in artificial intelligence and computer programming. Midlands Tech is proud to be able to educate so many different types of people.

Dr. Leroy Brown is proud of his accomplishments at Midlands Tech. "I felt that intellectually or mentally one could still be enslaved. Therefore I sought to . . . help others realize the potential of higher education." Thanks to schools like Midlands Tech, and to people like Dr. Leroy Brown, everyone can learn to keep up with the fast pace of the information age.

History to Inspire the Future

Founded in 1670, South Carolina's famous city of Charleston is one of the oldest cities in the South. It is also one of the oldest cultural centers of the nation. Almost every area of the arts had an early start in Charleston. The Dock Street Theater, the first playhouse in America, opened in 1736 and still presents performances. The city's literary culture got its start in 1748 with the opening of the Charleston Library Society. Charleston's musical society, the St. Cecilia Society, was established in 1762 as the first official organization in the nation to support music. Charleston also has the oldest public museum in the country, the Charleston Museum. It was founded in 1773, and visitors today still marvel at its natural history exhibits and its collection of area artifacts.

Over eight hundred of Charleston's buildings were constructed before the Civil War. Historic sites such as early plantations and the Civil War's Fort Sumter still add cultural flavor to the area. Charleston's golden age of the eighteenth century may be over, but many still

Catfish Row is a historic section of Charleston where people once sold goods from wheeled carts. Specialty shops now line the street.

above. Charleston, Columbia, and Greenville all host their own ballet companies.

below. Fort Sumter, the location of the first Civil War battle, has been restored and is now under the care of the National Park Service.

consider the town the cultural center of the South. One example of its continuing artistic leadership is the Spoleto Festival. Every May, Charleston exchanges artists with the town of Spoleto, Italy, for an extravaganza of over one hundred music, theater, dance, art, and film events.

Charleston and its nearby cities aren't the only source of culture in South Carolina. Folk arts such as weaving, quilt making, traditional songs, and dancing have been thriving in the state for many generations. Many African American communities on the islands around Charleston Harbor are centers of folk crafts. The Blue Ridge Mountains, in the western part of the state, boast some of the finest fiddlers and banjo pickers in the nation.

Famous artists of all types have come out of South Carolina. One of the best jazz trumpeters in the world, Dizzy Gillespie, is from the small town of Cheraw. Born John Birks Gillespie, he helped create a style of jazz called "bebop" in the 1940s and 1950s.

Many famous writers were also raised in South Carolina. George Gershwin based his great American opera *Porgy and Bess* on the novel *Porgy* by DuBose Heyward, a South Carolinian writer. The story took place on a Charleston waterfront street called Catfish Row. Julia Peterkin won the Pulitzer Prize in 1929 for her novel *Scarlet Sister Mary*. The book detailed the life of poor African Americans in the eastern area of the state called the Low Country.

Who knows what artists are still waiting to emerge from South Carolina? A program called Arts Education Initiatives (AEI) is cultivating the arts in schools all across the state. AEI arranges for all kinds of artists—dancers, actors, writers, musicians, visual artists, and folk artists— to visit a school for one week. During their visits, they work with students, teaching their artistic specialty and organizing a final presentation or performance. After an artist's visit, the program helps the school to develop the creative seeds planted by the visiting artist.

South Carolina is proud of its colorful and varied culture. Its active support of the arts promises to keep the state culturally rich for years to come.

above. Dizzy Gillespie, one of the fathers of bebop, was known for clowning around on stage and for his famous bent trumpet. The trumpet wasn't bent by design— someone sat on it!

below. Charleston's Dock Street Theatre was the first playhouse in the nation. The building originally housed the Planter's Hotel, built in 1809.

A Sea Island Story

Off the coasts of Georgia and South Carolina is a low-lying chain of sandy islands called the Sea Islands. The Gullah are the descendants of people brought to the Sea Islands to work as slaves on the cotton and rice plantations. In the days before the Civil War, the growers often spent up to six months a year away from their plantations. The Gullah, left alone and separated from the mainland, developed their own culture and language. Much of this culture was based on their West African ancestry. Their customs and beliefs can be traced to the Ibo, Yoruba, Kongo, Mandinka, and other West African cultures.

The American Civil War left the South economically devastated. By 1870 most of the Sea Island plantations were abandoned, and the Gullah set up small family farms on the land. For about a century, the Gullah have been living on the islands apart from American culture and modern technology. Their culture is held together by close-knit extended families. Their skills, folktales, laws, and overall culture have evolved over generations.

The Gullah language is a mixture of seventeenth-century English and various West African languages. It is spoken rapidly and many of the original English words have been shortened. For example, the Gullah say *E* to mean "he," "she," and "it." *Shum* is a combination of the words "see" or "saw," and "him," "her," "it," or "them." In many cases, the meaning of the sentence can only be taken from the context of the statement. The sentence *E fa go shum* may mean a number of things. Literally, the sentence may mean "He take go see her" or "He went to see her." However, depending on the subject, the sentence may mean instead "She went to see it."

Many of the Sea Islands have enchanting names, such as Daufuskie, Dewees, Tybee, Wassaw, Ossabaw, and Sapelo. The Sea Islands themselves may seem enchanting to those who have never visited them, but for the Gullah it is another story. Developers have been building high-rise hotels, condominiums, and golf courses on some of these islands since the

1950s. And more development is in the planning stages. On Daufuskie the development is expected to push the permanent population to ten thousand residents. In 1980 its mainly Gullah population totaled only 59. Whether or not the Gullah can maintain their unique language and culture among the influences of modern America is a question that remains to be answered.

Family is important to the Gullah, all of whom, however young, are expected to know their family history.

The Sea Islands are becoming more and more developed with resort areas like this one. As a result, most Gullah have two names—the name used by people they trust, and the name they tell to strangers.

A Foothold on the Future

South Carolina is well prepared for the future. Service industries are increasing employment opportunities. Agriculture has varied its crops so that a disaster like the boll weevil invasion of cotton in the 1920s won't destroy the whole industry. The state's manufacturing base is also solid, especially with the help of its strong roots in foreign trade. But there are still some adjustments South Carolinians are making as they move ahead into the twenty-first century.

First of all, South Carolina plans to expand its industry and make it more varied, as it has done with agriculture. The textile and chemical industries are especially strong, but they cannot provide all the jobs the state needs. The increasing use of high technology in factories makes production more efficient, but too often people are replaced with machines. Job training programs are working well to retrain workers who have lost their jobs. But there still need to be more opportunities for the growing number of people in the state.

South Carolina's tourist industry should continue to thrive in places such as Myrtle Beach.

In addition, more industry means more danger to the environment. The state legislature and community groups have taken steps to protect endangered species, such as the bald eagle and the alligator. Air and water pollution are on the rise, however.

South Carolina also needs to continue improving life outside its cities. Many rural residents have missed out on help that the state has given to urban areas, including better health and education programs. Increasing the reach of these programs will ensure that no one gets left behind.

"While I breathe, I hope," says South Carolina's state motto. The state is far from out of breath. Once South Carolina translates its hope into action, its future will be virtually limitless.

Unlike other sea turtles, loggerhead turtles are not an endangered species. However, they still are threatened by human hunters, who want the turtles and their eggs for food and also for their shells, hides, and oil.

Important Historical Events

1521 Spanish explorers from Santo Domingo are the first Europeans to enter the area.

1526 A temporary Spanish settlement is established at the mouth of Winyah Bay.

1562 A short-lived French settlement is established on Parris Island.

1629 King Charles I gives the land called *Carolana* to Sir Robert Heath.

1663 King Charles II gives *Carolana* to the eight lords proprietor.

1670 Charles Towne is founded at Albemarle Point.

1680 Charles Towne moves to the present site of Charleston.

1715 The Yamassee War begins.

1719 The colonists rebel against the lords proprietor. King George makes South Carolina a royal colony.

1736 The Dock Street Theater opens in Charleston.

1776 The British are defeated in an attempt to occupy Charleston.

1780 South Carolina patriots defeat the British at Kings Mountain.

1781 The British are defeated at Cowpens.

1788 South Carolina enters the Union as the eighth state.

1828 South Carolinian Andrew Jackson becomes the seventh President of the United States.

1830 The first working steam locomotive in the United States makes its first run out of Charleston.

1832 South Carolina adopts the Ordinance of Nullification, declaring two federal tax laws null and void.

1860 South Carolina is the first state to withdraw from the Union.

1861 Confederate troops fire on Fort Sumter.

1865 General William Sherman burns many plantations and towns in South Carolina, including Columbia.

1868 South Carolina is readmitted to the Union.

1890 Benjamin Tillman is elected governor. He takes away the rights of African Americans, including the right to vote.

1920s The boll weevil destroys half of the state's cotton crop.

1948 The right to vote is returned to African Americans in South Carolina.

1955 The South Carolina legislature repeals its law that children have to attend school.

1967 The South Carolina legislature requires children to attend school again.

1970 South Carolina and the city of Charleston celebrate their three hundredth anniversary.

1983 I. DeQuincey Newman is elected to the State Senate.

1988 Three nuclear reactors in Aiken are shut down for safety reasons.

1989 Hurricane Hugo hits South Carolina, killing 180 people.

1992 BMW, the European automaker, announces plans to build an assembly plant in South Carolina. It would be the company's first United States production plant.

45

The state flag shows a palmetto tree and a crescent moon. The palmetto is the state tree and the symbol of the defense of Sullivans Island. The island fort was made from palmetto logs.

South Carolina Almanac

Nickname. The Palmetto State

Capital. Columbia

State Bird. Carolina wren

State Flower. Yellow jessamine

State Tree. Palmetto

State Mottoes. *Animis opibusque parati* (Prepared in Mind and Resources) and *Dum spiro spero* (While I Breathe, I Hope)

State Songs. "Carolina" and "South Carolina on My Mind"

State Abbreviations. S.C. (traditional); SC (postal)

Statehood. May 23, 1788, the eighth state

Government. Congress: U.S. senators, 2; U.S. representatives, 6. State Legislature: senators, 46; representatives, 124. Counties: 46

Area. 31,113 sq mi (80,582 sq km), 40th in size among the states

Greatest Distances. north/south, 218 mi (351 km); east/west, 275 mi (443 km). Coastline: 187 mi (301 km)

Elevation. Highest: Sassafras Mountain, 3,560 ft (1,085 m). Lowest: sea level, along the Atlantic Ocean

Population. 1990 Census: 3,505,707 (12% increase over 1980), 25th in size among the states. Density: 113 persons per sq mi (43 persons per sq km). Distribution: 55% urban, 45% rural. 1980 Census: 3,112,814

Economy. *Agriculture:* tobacco, corn, soybeans, cotton, peaches, beef cattle. *Fishing:* shrimp, crabs, clams, oysters. *Manufacturing:* textiles, chemical products, paper products, machinery. *Mining:* limestone, granite, clay, cement

State Seal

State Flower: Yellow jessamine

State Bird: Carolina wren

Annual Events

★ Africa Alive in Rock Hill (February)

★ Governor's Frog Jump and Egg Striking Contest in Springfield (April)

★ Stone Soup Storytelling Festival in Woodruff (April)

★ Gullah Festival in Beaufort (May)

★ Spoleto Festival USA in Charleston (May)

★ Sun-Fun Festival in Myrtle Beach (June)

★ Railroad Festival in Central (September)

★ Southern 500 NASCAR stock car race in Darlington (September)

★ Ghost Tour in Georgetown (October)

★ State Fair in Columbia (October)

★ Chitlin' Strut in Salley (November)

Places to Visit

★ Carowinds theme park, near Rock Hill

★ Charleston Museum

★ Cherokee Foothills Scenic Highway through the western mountain region

★ Cowpens National Battlefield in Cherokee County

★ Cypress Gardens, near Charleston

★ Fort Moultrie and Fort Sumter in Charleston Harbor

★ Francis Marion National Forest, near Charleston

★ NMPA Stock Car Hall of Fame in Darlington

★ Seaside Resorts such as Hilton Head and Myrtle Beach

★ Secession Hill and Burt-Stark House in Abbeville

Index